THE CHICAGO BEARS

BY THOMAS K. ADAMSON

EPIC

BELLWETHER MEDIA ★ MINNEAPOLIS, MN

EPIC BOOKS are no ordinary books. They burst with intense action, high-speed heroics, and shadows of the unknown. Are you ready for an Epic adventure?

This book is intended for educational use. Organization and franchise logos are trademarks of the National Football League (NFL). This is not an official book of the NFL. It is not approved by or connected with the NFL.

This edition first published in 2024 by Bellwether Media, Inc.

No part of this publication may be reproduced in whole or in part without written permission of the publisher. For information regarding permission, write to Bellwether Media, Inc., Attention: Permissions Department, 6012 Blue Circle Drive, Minnetonka, MN 55343.

Library of Congress Cataloging-in-Publication Data

Names: Adamson, Thomas K., 1970- author.
Title: The Chicago Bears / by Thomas K. Adamson.
Description: Minneapolis, MN : Bellwether Media, 2024. | Series: Epic. NFL team profiles | Includes bibliographical references and index. | Audience: Ages 7-12 | Audience: Grades 2-3 | Summary: "Engaging images accompany information about the Chicago Bears. The combination of high-interest subject matter and light text is intended for students in grades 2 through 7"-- Provided by publisher.
Identifiers: LCCN 2023021293 (print) | LCCN 2023021294 (ebook) | ISBN 9798886874716 (library binding) | ISBN 9798886876598 (ebook)
Subjects: LCSH: Chicago Bears (Football team)--History--Juvenile literature.
Classification: LCC GV956.C5 A43 2024 (print) | LCC GV956.C5 (ebook) | DDC 796.332/640977311--dc23/eng/20230517
LC record available at https://lccn.loc.gov/2023021293
LC ebook record available at https://lccn.loc.gov/2023021294

Text copyright © 2024 by Bellwether Media, Inc. EPIC and associated logos are trademarks and/or registered trademarks of Bellwether Media, Inc.

Editor: Elizabeth Neuenfeldt   Designer: Gabriel Hilger

Printed in the United States of America, North Mankato, MN.

TABLE OF CONTENTS

SUPER RETURN	4
THE HISTORY OF THE BEARS	6
THE BEARS TODAY	14
GAME DAY!	16
CHICAGO BEARS FACTS	20
GLOSSARY	22
TO LEARN MORE	23
INDEX	24

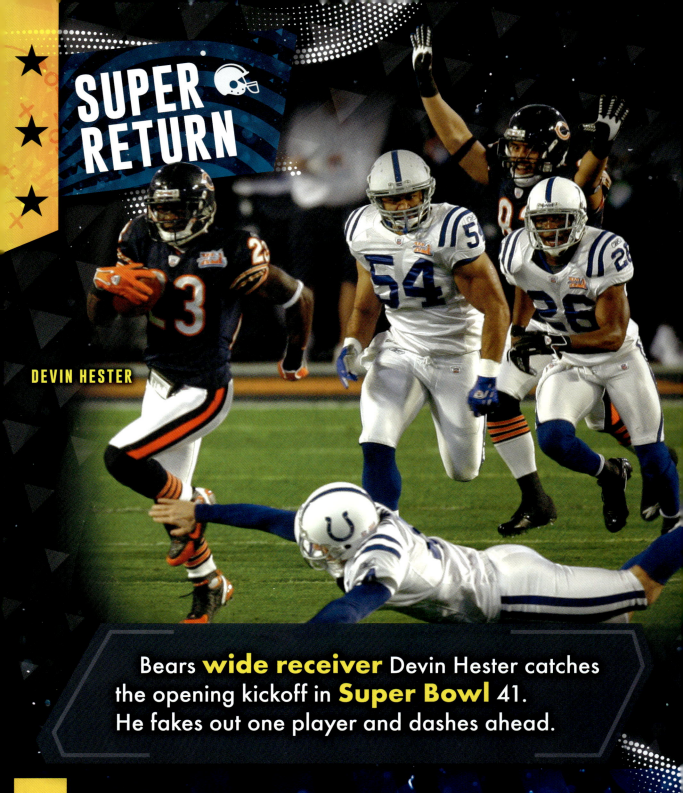

SUPER RETURN

DEVIN HESTER

Bears **wide receiver** Devin Hester catches the opening kickoff in **Super Bowl** 41. He fakes out one player and dashes ahead.

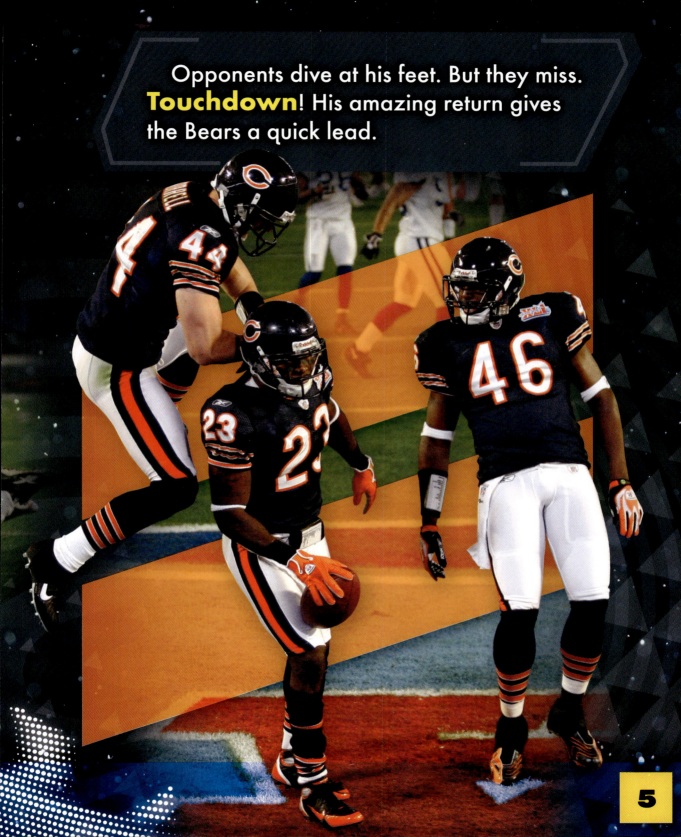

Opponents dive at his feet. But they miss. **Touchdown**! His amazing return gives the Bears a quick lead.

THE HISTORY OF THE BEARS

The Chicago Bears are among the oldest teams in the National Football League (NFL). They began in 1920 in Decatur, Illinois. They were called the Staleys.

In 1921, they moved to Chicago, Illinois. In 1922, the team was renamed the Bears.

1920 DECATUR STALEYS

STALEY STARCH
The Staleys were named after the Staley starch company.

CHICAGO, ILLINOIS

The Bears' first coach was George Halas. He was known for the **T formation offense**. It kept other teams guessing.

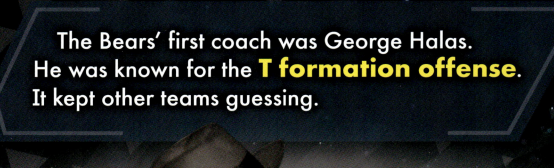

GEORGE HALAS

RUNNING UP THE SCORE
The Bears won the biggest blowout in NFL history. They beat Washington 73-0 in the 1940 NFL Championship Game!

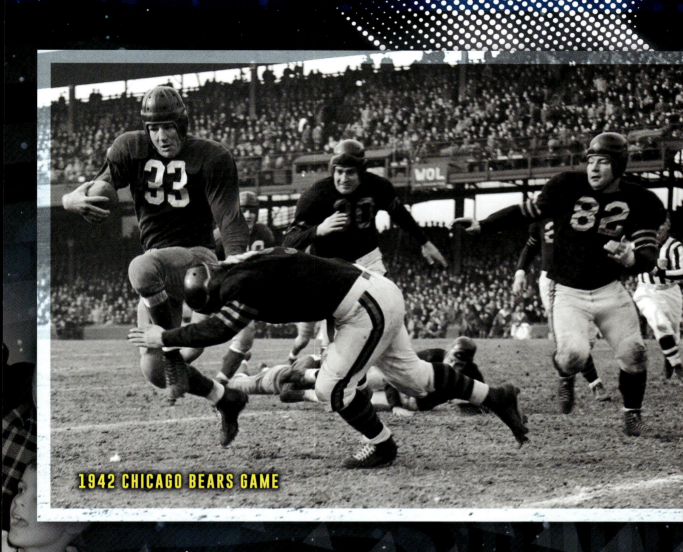

1942 CHICAGO BEARS GAME

The Bears had the best record of the 1940s. Their strong **defense** earned them the nickname Monsters of the Midway.

The Bears struggled in the 1950s. They won the NFL **championship** in 1963. But they had little success after that.

MIKE DITKA

SUPER BOWL SHUFFLE

In 1985, Bears players recorded the song "The Super Bowl Shuffle." The song proudly stated they would win the Super Bowl.

In 1975, **running back** Walter Payton joined the team. Later, Mike Ditka became head coach. The 1985 team won Super Bowl 20!

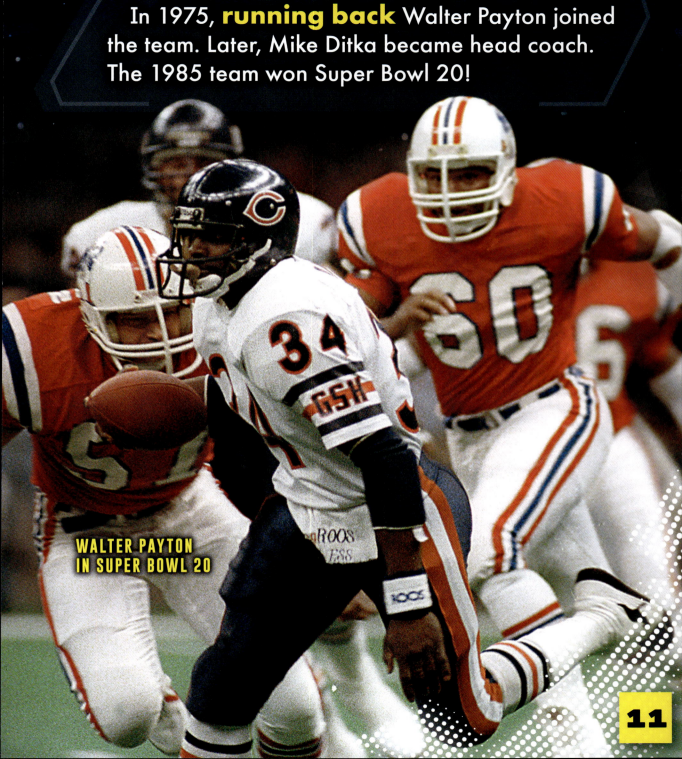

WALTER PAYTON IN SUPER BOWL 20

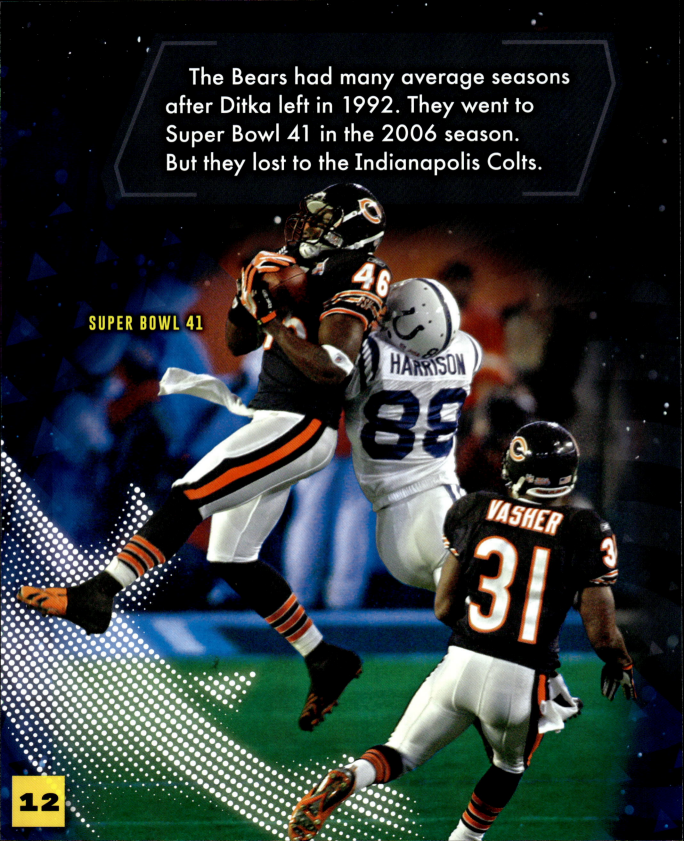

The Bears had many average seasons after Ditka left in 1992. They went to Super Bowl 41 in the 2006 season. But they lost to the Indianapolis Colts.

SUPER BOWL 41

The Bears struggled in the 2010s. They only reached the **playoffs** twice.

TROPHY CASE

- **NFC NORTH championships:** 3
- **NFC championships:** 2
- **SUPER BOWL championships:** 1
- **NFL championships:** 8

THE BEARS TODAY

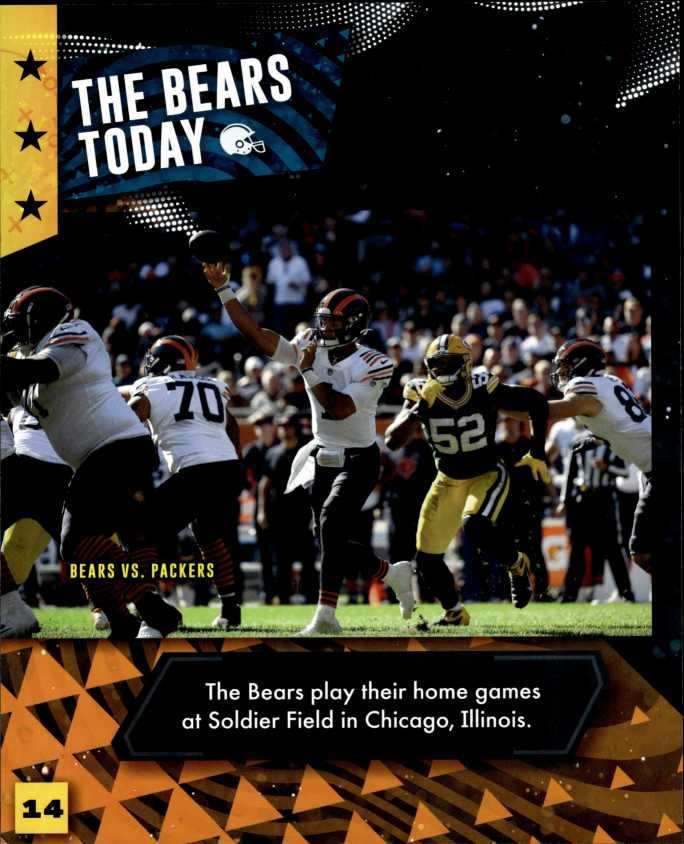

BEARS VS. PACKERS

The Bears play their home games at Soldier Field in Chicago, Illinois.

The team plays in the NFC North **division**. Their **rivalry** with the Green Bay Packers is over 100 years old.

📍 LOCATION 📍

SOLDIER FIELD
Chicago, Illinois

ILLINOIS

GAME DAY!

The Bears' **mascot** is Staley Da Bear. He cheers with fans at home games. Many Bears fans get ready for games by **tailgating**. Before home games, fans get together, eat food, and play games.

TAILGATING

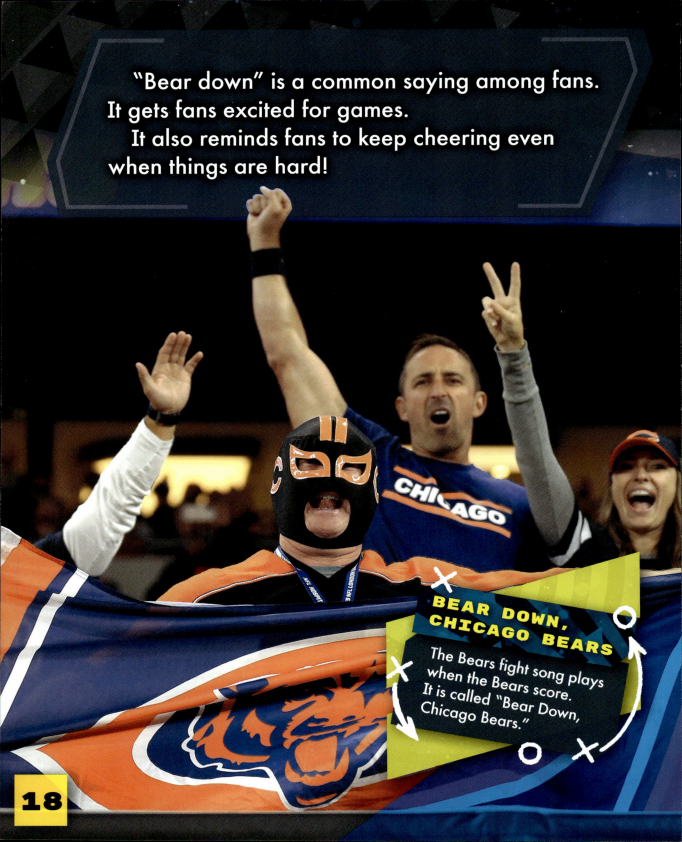

"Bear down" is a common saying among fans. It gets fans excited for games.
It also reminds fans to keep cheering even when things are hard!

BEAR DOWN, CHICAGO BEARS

The Bears fight song plays when the Bears score. It is called "Bear Down, Chicago Bears."

★ FAMOUS PLAYERS ★

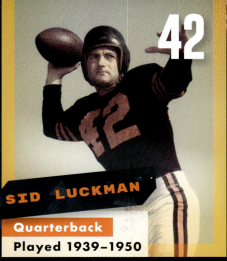

42

SID LUCKMAN

Quarterback
Played 1939–1950

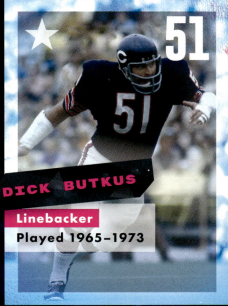

51

DICK BUTKUS

Linebacker
Played 1965–1973

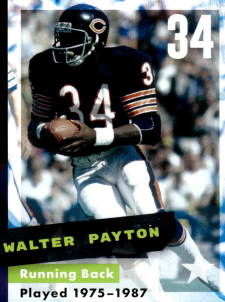

34

WALTER PAYTON

Running Back
Played 1975–1987

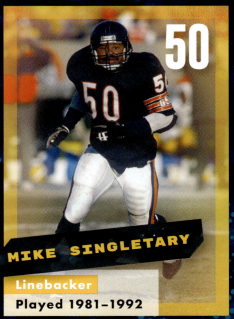

50

MIKE SINGLETARY

Linebacker
Played 1981–1992

54

BRIAN URLACHER

Linebacker
Played 2000–2012

CHICAGO BEARS FACTS

LOGO

JOINED THE NFL | **1920**

NICKNAME | Monsters of the Midway

MASCOT — STALEY DA BEAR

CONFERENCE | National Football Conference (NFC)

COLORS

DIVISION | NFC North

 Detroit Lions
 Green Bay Packers
 Minnesota Vikings

STADIUM

★ **SOLDIER FIELD** ★
opened October 9, 1924

holds **63,500** people

⏱ TIMELINE

1920 The team forms as the Decatur Staleys

1921 The team moves to Chicago and later becomes the Bears

1975 Walter Payton joins the Bears

1986 The Bears win Super Bowl 20

2007 The Bears play in Super Bowl 41

★ RECORDS ★

All-Time Rushing Leader

Walter Payton
16,726 yards

All-Time Punt Return Touchdowns Leader

 Devin Hester
13 touchdowns

All-Time Passing Leader
 Jay Cutler
23,443 yards

Single-Season Receiving Leader

Brandon Marshall
1,508 yards in 2012

GLOSSARY

championship—a contest to decide the best team or person

defense—the group of players who try to stop the opposing team from scoring

division—a group of NFL teams from the same area that often play against each other; there are eight divisions in the NFL.

mascot—an animal or symbol that represents a sports team

playoffs—games played after the regular season is over; playoff games determine which teams play in the championship game.

rivalry—the state of having a long-standing opponent

running back—a player whose main job is to run with the ball

Super Bowl—the annual championship game of the NFL

T formation offense—a football formation in which the running backs line up behind the quarterback

tailgating—having a party in the parking lot at a sporting event

touchdown—a score that occurs when a team crosses into their opponent's end zone with the football; a touchdown is worth six points.

wide receiver—a player whose main job is to catch passes from the quarterback

TO LEARN MORE

AT THE LIBRARY

Abdo, Kenny. *Chicago Bears.* Minneapolis, Minn.: Abdo Zoom, 2022.

Ellenport, Craig. *The Story of the Chicago Bears.* Minneapolis, Minn.: Kaleidoscope, 2020.

Hill, Christina. *Inside the Chicago Bears.* Minneapolis, Minn.: Lerner Publications, 2023.

ON THE WEB

FACTSURFER

Factsurfer.com gives you a safe, fun way to find more information.

1. Go to www.factsurfer.com.

2. Enter "Chicago Bears" into the search box and click 🔍.

3. Select your book cover to see a list of related content.

INDEX

Chicago, Illinois, 6, 7, 14, 15
Chicago Bears facts, 20–21
colors, 20
Decatur, Illinois, 6
defense, 9
Ditka, Mike, 10, 11, 12
famous players, 19
fans, 16, 18
Halas, George, 8
Hester, Devin, 4, 5
history, 4, 5, 6, 7, 8, 9, 10, 11, 12, 13, 15
mascot, 16, 17, 20
name, 6, 7
National Football League (NFL), 6, 8, 10, 20
NFC North, 15, 20
NFL Championship Game, 8, 10
nickname, 9, 20
Payton, Walter, 11
playoffs, 13
positions, 4, 11
records, 8, 9, 21
rivalry, 15
Soldier Field, 14, 15, 20
songs, 10, 18
Super Bowl, 4, 5, 10, 11, 12
T formation offense, 8
tailgating, 16
timeline, 21
trophy case, 13

The images in this book are reproduced through the courtesy of: Kara Durrette/ AP Images, cover (hero); Thomas Barrat, cover (stadium); Tribune Content Agency LLC/ Alamy, p. 3; Kevork Djansezian/ AP Images, pp. 4, 5; ASSOCIATED PRESS/ AP Images, p. 6; Joseph Sohm, pp. 6-7; Bettmann/ Contributor/ Getty, pp. 8, 9, 19 (Sid Luckman), 21 (1975); Jewell/ AP Images, p. 10; RED MCLENDON/ AP Images, pp. 10-11; Zuma Press Inc./ Alamy, p. 12; Quinn Harris/ Stringer/ Getty, p. 14; marchello74, p. 15 (Soldier Field); NFL/ Wikipedia, pp. 15 (Chicago Bears logo), 19 (Chicago Bears logo, Detroit Lions logo, Green Bay Packers logo, Minnesota Vikings logo, NFC logo), 21 (1920); Kena Krutsinger/ Stringer/ Getty, p. 16; Icon Sportswire/ Getty, pp. 16-17; Tottenham Hotspur FC/ Contributor/ Getty, pp. 18-19; Focus On Sport/ Contributor/ Getty, pp. 19 (Dick Butkus, Walter Payton, Mike Singletary), 21 (1986); Jonathan Daniel/ Staff/ Getty, p. 19 (Brian Urlacher); Dilip Vishwanat/ Contributor/ Getty, p. 20 (mascot); Richard Cavalleri, p. 20 (stadium); Sean Pavone, p. 21 (1921); Eliot J. Schechter/ Stringer/ Getty, p. 21 (2007); James Biever Photography LLC/ Contributor, p. 21 (Walter Payton); UPI/ Alamy, p. 21 (Devin Hester); Jonathan Daniel/ Staff/ Getty, p. 21 (Jay Cutler, Brandon Marshall); Emilee Chinn/ Stringer/ Getty, p. 23.